DO CHRISTIANS HATE?

The world says we do;

The Word says we do;

But . . .

A Biblical perspective

Jonathan Rupprecht

Lutheran News, Inc.
New Haven, Missouri

Do Christians Hate?
Copyright (c) 2019 Lutheran News, Inc. All Rights Reserved. No portion of this book may be reproduced in any form, except for quotations in reviews, articles, and speeches, without permisison from the publisher.

Library of Congress Card
Lutheran News, Inc.
684 Luther Lane
New Haven, MO 63068
Published 2019
Printed in the United States of America
IngramSpark, TN
ISBN #

CONTENTS

Introduction	page i
The world says we do	page 1
Love is foundational	page 2
The Word says we do	page 4
We hate the world	page 6
The world hates us	page 7
The negative Christian	page 8
That critical balance	page 10
Hatred and homosexuality	page 11
Hatred and Islam	page 14
Hatred and evolution	page 16
No, it's not political	page 18
Appreciate the contrast	page 19
Misplaced compassion	page 20
The threats and our response	page 21
What are we known for?	page 23
Summary	page 24
Further resources	page 25

INTRODUCTION

" 'Do Christians hate?' What kind of question is that? Of course Christians don't hate; Christians love! The Christian faith is about God's love for us! And He tells us over and over again to reflect to each other His love for us, to love all people, to love even our enemies. 'Do Christians hate?' Why on earth do you ask such a ridiculous question?"

Because it's not ridiculous. It might sound that way at first, and many people will say it is and react as just described. But it takes more than a quick, superficial reaction to properly address and answer this timely and important question. When giving it further consideration, we realize that not only does the world around us accuse us of hating, but we discover that God Himself *instructs* us to hate! The first part is frustrating and even threatening; the second part can be puzzling and complicated. So we need to take a closer look at this whole key issue and see what is really involved for us when asking, "Do Christians hate?" This will also help to fine-tune our *apologetics*: our words and actions in defense of the faith.

THE WORLD SAYS WE DO

The impetus for this consideration comes from the societal environment in which we live today. If we give that context even some brief thought, it is easy to realize what is behind this study. Issues and charges of hatred fill the air more than at any time in memory. While the term "hate crimes" was reported as far back as 1959 in the popular exposé *"Black Like Me"* by journalist John Howard Griffin, in late 2018 the FBI tabulated a 17% increase in hate crimes for 2017. Along with that term, two other increasingly prevalent terms and their threats come to mind: "hate speech" and "hate groups". All three terms have been applied to us as Christians. Since we would normally see hatred as an alien emotion, so to speak, we need to carefully come to grips with these issues, these charges. How do they impact our Christian lives? How do we respond to that impact? Do Christians hate? The world says we do; the Word says we do. ***But . . .***

A disclaimer is important to start with. The issue here is not God's standard, familiar prohibitions of personal hatred, best summed up in I John 3:15 – *"Whoever hates his brother is a murderer, and you know that no murder has eternal life in him."* Thus in our cultural climate today, we need to be clear up front that this study in no way identifies with the unChristian hatred that so often seems to dominate the news. We are not remotely close to endorsing or indulging in the kind of hatred that is often behind the increasing domestic terror and mass shootings today, the hatred we often encounter from socio-political groups on the right or left, or anything in between. We are dealing with strictly Scriptural considerations and how they are to be manifested in our lives. We're striving to make timely applications of God's timeless truths.

LOVE IS FOUNDATIONAL

To do so, it is only right that we first review the fundamental aspect that the objection above deals with: love, not hatred, is foundational to the Christian faith and life. We think of familiar and beloved Bible passages such as John 3:16, probably the most frequently quoted passage in all of Scripture: *"God so loved the world that He gave His one and only Son, that whoever believes in Him shall not perish but have eternal life."* Or 1 John 4:9&10 – *"This is how God showed His love among us: He sent His one and only Son into the world that we might live through Him. This is love: not that we loved God but that He loved us and sent His Son as an atoning sacrifice for our sins."* Scripture abounds with God's testimonies to His amazing, undeserved love for us sinners.

And our loving response to this love from God is also clearly laid out for us. For example, St. John writes,

> *"Dear friends, since God so loved us, we also ought to love one another. . . . We know and rely on the love God has for us. God is love. Whoever lives in love lives in God, and God in him. In this way love is made complete among us . . . . We love because He first loved us. . . . Whoever loves God must also love his brother."* (1 John 4:11, 16, 17, 19, 21).
>
> John also quotes Jesus: *"A new command I give you: Love one another. As I have loved you, so you must love one another. By this all men will know that you are My disciples, if you love one another."* (John 13:34&35).

Read for yourself how Jesus elaborates on this in John 15:9-17.

And as mentioned above, our Lord Jesus tells us to love even our enemies:
> *"Love your enemies; pray for those who persecute you, that you may be children of your Father in heaven."* (Matthew 5:44&45)

Beautiful, moving words, at the heart of the Christian faith and life. Yet God also makes very clear the inevitable corollary to this story of His love and ours. When anything or anyone obstructs, contradicts, ignores, denies, defies what our loving Lord does for us and says to us, the loving Christian has a reaction quite the opposite of our reaction to God's love.

This is both natural and Scriptural. It makes sense, common sense, to start with: if we love peace, we hate war; if we love it when our team wins, we hate it when our team loses; if we love warm sunshine, we hate cold dreariness; and so on. But of course we need to progress beyond mere human common sense to Biblical sense, to God's will for our reactions. In this broad issue at least, our God-directed emotions, so far beyond mere human reactions, are a binary matter. When we fear and love the Lord, we will hate whatever opposes Him. And we not only *will* do so, we *are to* do so, as we'll see. Yes, Christians *should* hate; God says so!

THE WORD SAYS WE DO

Maybe the most simple and familiar Bible passage to summarize this important point is Proverbs 8:13 – *"To fear the Lord is to hate evil."* Notice there the word "is". To fear the Lord does not *possibly involve* hating evil; it *is* to hate evil. The two opposite responses just go together; two inseparable parts of the whole. For anyone who fears the Lord it is necessary, inevitable to hate evil. And this is a theme throughout Scripture.

For example, we read almost the very same words in Psalm 97:10 – *"Let those who love the Lord hate evil."*

In Psalm 119 the Psalmist writes, *"I gain understanding from Your precepts; therefore I hate every wrong path. . . . I hate and abhor falsehood but I love Your law."* (vv. 104 & 163)

In Psalm 139 David writes, *"If only You would slay the wicked, O God! Away from me, you bloodthirsty men! They speak of You with evil intent; Your adversaries misuse Your name. Do I not hate those who hate You, O Lord, and abhor those who rise up against You?"* (vv. 19-21) How applicable these words are in our day and age! But we need to be careful and Biblical as we apply them to our own situations, as we'll see.

The Prophet Amos, in calling God's people to repentance, says, *"Hate evil, love good; maintain justice in the courts. Perhaps the Lord God Almighty will have mercy on the remnant of Joseph."* (5:15)

In the New Testament St. Paul repeats this theme in writing to the Christians in Rome: *"Love must be sincere. Hate what is evil, cling to what is good."* (12:9)

When he writes to the Galatians about the false doctrine that was attacking their faith, St. Paul makes this point with the utmost severity: *"Even if we or an angel from heaven should preach a gospel other than the one we preached to you, let him be eternally condemned! As we have already said, so now I say again: If anybody is preaching to you a gospel other than what you accepted, let him be eternally condemned!"* "Holy hatred" for sure! Shocking to those who don't or won't understand, but very instructive to those who love the Lord and His holy, saving Word.

This holy hatred in God's people simply mirrors the holy hatred of our loving Savior Himself. In Hebrews the writer applies the prophetic words of Psalm 45:7 to Jesus: *"You have loved righteousness and hated wickedness; therefore God Your God has set You above Your companions by anointing You with the oil of joy."* (1:9)

Words such as the quotations above are unfamiliar to many who know the Bible only superficially. But they are also unpopular, sometimes even repulsive, to many who know Scripture enough to encounter such passages on occasion. Furthermore, there are those who have a full working knowledge of Scripture who nevertheless ignore, even reject the points made by these words. Such situations are what this writing seeks to address, as well as seeking to equip and encourage those who do not react in such wrong ways yet look for clarification on this larger issue.

While love is foundational to the Christian faith, we see in these passages and in other places throughout Scripture that this is not the whole story of our Christian life. Our role as Christians is not simply a matter of saying, *"Smile, Jesus loves you"*; God's Word and our Christian witness are both more complex than that. And while *"Hatred is a Christian Virtue"* won't work as a bumper sticker, nevertheless to live as Christians in our world today, to function as both salt and light, as our Savior directs us to do (Matthew 5:13-16), we need to be actively informed about these complexities and directly involved in dealing clearly with them. Jude writes, "I *urge you to contend for the faith that was once for all entrusted to the saints."* (v. 3) In that contending we come to grips with the issues of the day while grounded in God's Word, functioning as His *apologists*: defenders of the faith.

WE HATE THE WORLD

First of all, what do we mean by "the world"? Not the planet itself, of course. This term in the Bible refers to the unbelief and Godlessness that characterize so much of the non-Christian, sometimes anti-Christian majority that inhabits this planet. *"The children of this world"*, as they are called in Scripture (Luke 16:8), think, speak and live in opposition to our Lord Jesus and the Word of God; sometimes deliberately and defiantly, other times just reflexively, subconsciously, subtly, or subliminally.

The world says that we hate, and they're right, we do; we hate the world. What? Yes, we've got those Bible passages above here, but isn't it a counterproductive overstatement to assert that we hate the world? No; we just need to be careful in how we deal with that hatred – in our hearts and from our mouths. Consider these words: *"Do not love the world, or anything in the world. If anyone loves the world, the love of the Father is not in him."* (I John 2:15) Or more specifically, *"Don't you know that friendship with the world is hatred toward God? Anyone who chooses to be a friend of the world becomes an enemy of God."* (James 4:4) As Christians we recognize the devil, *the world*, and our sinful nature as the three basic enemies of our faith. A holy hatred toward each one of those three is essential for our very survival as we are inescapably engaged in our life-long battle against them. We'll take a look below at how this applies to three examples of *"anything in the world"*.

THE WORLD HATES US

The world certainly hates us as Christians, especially when we witness to God's truth. After all, the children of this world neither know nor like God's truth, because it removes their moral options and it eliminates the flexibility of their "do-it-yourself" approach to religion. God's truth puts the children of this world in a place of humble submission when they would rather flounder in their imagined freedom from divine authority. God's Gospel truth contradicts their imagined ability to make themselves good enough to stand before God, whoever he – or she! – might happen to be. The world echoes Pontius Pilate: *"What is truth?"* (John 18:38) And thus when we approach the children of this world and speak God's Word as absolute truth, they consider this to be hate speech and call it that.

The world seeks to destroy whoever and whatever contradicts or threatens their imagined freedom and security and their real pride. The world blasphemously presumes to judge God according to its own shifting standards; but God righteously pronounces His judgment on the world according to His absolute, timeless, divine standards. Who's going to come out on top there?

The world hates us to the extent that we live as Christians, that we function as the salt of the earth and let our light shine on its darkness. Jesus explained this very directly: *"Everyone who does evil hates the light, and will not come into the light for fear that his deeds will be exposed."* (John 3:20) And thus while we let our Gospel light shine, we cannot pretend to be – or imagine that we can be – close friends with the world *on its terms* – even though we *can* be *outwardly* friendly with children of this world. As we just heard from James, *"Friendship with the world is hatred toward God."* (4:4) *That* kind of hatred we dare *never* be guilty of! Yet that is a serious risk if we fear and resist being labeled as haters, especially when that labeling comes from those who don't have a clue about the Biblical teaching on hatred that we have seen here.

THE NEGATIVE CHRISTIAN

Our engagement in the life-long battle against the forces of evil is often seen as being "negative". That's a softer charge than being a hater, but it more frequently arises from within the church. It is an understandable criticism. After all, we properly want to be positive, and we certainly aren't being negative or hateful simply for the sake of being negative or hateful. We are to encourage each other, to lift each other up, and to share the Gospel, the most positive message of all by far. ***But* . . .** when we read Scripture we can't miss the fact that so much of it would have to be called "negative": dire warnings about false teachings and false teachers; serious repeated cautions about the devil's temptations and about our own sinful nature, and of course those prevalent, pointed lessons about the evils in the sinful world around us.

Our Lord expects us to take these loving warnings seriously; we are to *"fight the good fight of the faith"* (1 Timothy 6:12), and that cannot be done without an open, honest recognition of the powerful *negative* forces that threaten us, individually and together, and then positively confronting them. This confronting will typically come across as quite negative, and it will seem – and sometimes be – hateful, as explained above. ***But* . . .** we understand that explanation and need not hold back because of false accusations and misunderstandings. In heaven we will be the Church Triumphant, but here on earth we are the Church Militant: soldiers of the cross on active duty against the enemy, in defense of the faith and in service to our Lord and His people.

Children of this world use the term "hate" with no conception of the Scriptural context for the term. They project the view that all hatred is always completely evil and therefore must be combated. But of course their cries are anything but objective and fair, since in that process they hypocritically ignore the strident voices on their own side that often express truly ugly – and even Satanic - hatred of Christians and Christian values. Thus when such voices accuse us of hatred, we need to consider their source. And we need to recognize and reject the world's implication that there is a moral equivalence between their Godless hatred and our Godly hatred. They in fact have opposite sources and objects.

When particular evils arise in a prominent and dominant way in our world, our Christian voice – individually and collectively – dare not be silent, lest that silence be taken for tacit approval, consent. We rightly speak out in criticism of what is wrong, of what we hate because God hates it. This is righteous hatred, necessary criticism. The familiar words traditionally attributed to Edmund Burke come to mind: *"The only thing necessary for the triumph of evil is for good men to do nothing."* More to the point, our loving Lord hates it when His dear children fail to speak up as He wants us to do in such circumstances. He asks, *"Who will rise up for Me against the wicked? Who will take a stand for Me against evildoers?"* (Psalm 94:16) Such a stand is not a hate crime or even hate speech (the world's terms, not ours) but simply a faithful, necessary testimony to God's truth and a call to repentance.

In this connection, we need to be careful not to let the unbelieving world define the terms for us. Any time we speak up against a sinful issue, we are seen as being "negative"; we are called "haters" by the world – who hates us and our Lord and His Word! ***But . . .*** our words are simply *valid criticism* and *faithful testimony*. Even the children of this world exercise criticism and recognize its importance, validity, necessity. Criticisms of faulty products, incorrect analyses, dangerous proposals, etc., are ubiquitous. And any objective person recognizes that criticism and personal hatred are by no means synonymous.

THAT CRITICAL BALANCE

***But* . . .** this is where it can get a little complicated. We are often reminded that "it's not just *what* you say but *how* you say it." God Himself tells us this in Ephesians 4:15, that key verse where we are told to *"speak the truth in love"* – that is, in love for the truth, in love for the Lord whose truth it is, and also in love for the person or people to whom we speak it.

Personally, I become quite incensed at the flagrant defense and aggressive promotion of grossly sinful attitudes, anti-Scriptural ideologies, Godless lifestyles and the defiance of God in our world today. Yet when I interact in person with an individual who exemplifies or concurs with such attitudes and actions, I need to be very careful. Even in a case where it's clear that such a person is well aware of what Holy Scripture says about such matters yet lives and speaks in opposition to it anyway, I still need initially to approach lovingly, address carefully and testify patiently to this person unless or until the point comes where his or her persistent defiance and possible threats bring into play a clear application of Jesus' directive: *"If anyone will not . . . listen to your words, shake the dust off your feet when you leave"* (Matthew 10:14).

But until that point, and in general situations, the Lord has given me this contact, this opportunity, to win this person for His kingdom. And as the saying goes, *"you'll catch more flies with honey than with vinegar"*; I'll need to speak God's truth in love for that person, a blood-bought soul.

HATRED AND HOMOSEXUALITY

Let's take for an example a major societal and spiritual factor today: homosexuality and its attendant issues such as so-called "gay marriage" and the whole transgender scenario. We often hear the saying, "God hates the sin but loves the sinner." While these words have sometimes been misused to soften God's righteous hatred of sin, Scripture does express this contrast. For example, in Romans 5:8 we read, *"God demonstrates His own love for us in this: while we were still sinners, Christ died for us."* Yet we also have passages such as Psalm 5: 5 – *"You hate all who do wrong"* – which show us that God has what we might call a love/hate relationship with us as sinners. This of course is nothing but that basic Biblical duality of law and gospel. So keeping that critical Scriptural balance in mind, "God hates the sin but loves the sinner" can serve as a helpful approach and model for us in dealing with our righteous hatred and voicing our dutiful criticism here. How do we properly apply that balance in this issue?

Let's first address the term "homophobia". Its literal meaning is *fear of* homosexuals. The world accuses confessional Christians of homophobia, but that's as misleading as the world's purposeful juxtaposition of "hatred" for "criticism". We don't fear homosexuals as such, but we are very concerned about what the growing acceptance and sanctioning of everything homosexual is doing to the world we live in and to so much of the Christian church. But of course when the world accuses us of homophobia, their real intent is to accuse us of a hate crime against homosexuals. This is not true, **but . . .**

It is often said that we shouldn't single out homosexuality for special condemnation; after all, any and all sins condemn us before God. This is most certainly true, yet it's not the whole truth concerning this matter. For one thing, homosexuality has become a major social, Biblical issue in the world of our day that inescapably necessitates our involved reaction as Christians. The so-called "homosexual agenda" dominates the discussion of these issues in our world. Homosexuality is approved, and any disapproving voices are called hate speech, even hate crimes. Homosexuality is not just acknowledged as legitimate, but legislation and public opinion are pushed energetically in that direction, with special favors for LGBT voices. Homosexual public figures have been highlighted as a combination of victims and heroes, and the entire deviant transgender issue is aggressively and sympathetically pursued. And although "gay marriage" was never previously granted official, legal approval by any civilized – or uncivilized – society, yet it now is not just officially sanctioned by the US Supreme Court, but reportedly supported by a solid and growing majority of American citizens.

Also, God does single out homosexual sins for special treatment in His Word. In the Old Testament His description of homosexuality is translated as *"detestable"*, *"disgusting"*, or *"abominable"*, and deserving the death penalty (Leviticus 20:13); and in the New Testament His describing term for it is sometimes translated as *"perversion"* (Romans 1:27, Jude 7), thus providing a special negative niche apart from God's typical terminology for more "ordinary" sins such as lying, stealing, even murder. Homosexuality is portrayed as a special affront to God, as we see in the unique and severe judgment He rained down because of it on Sodom and Gomorrah (Genesis 19). In Matthew chapters 10 and 11 Jesus twice cites Sodom as the example of God's most severe, dramatic, memorable judgment. And Christian historians have seen the general acceptance of homosexuality as a common – even if not immediately inevitable – sign of decay in a civilization.

Thus as God's children we need to recognize both God's view of this category of sins and also what its approval is doing to not only the moral climate of the world we live in but also to that unfortunately large portion of Christianity that wrongly sympathizes with the world's take on this matter and ignores or "adjusts" God's Word to accommodate the "politically correct" views of the day.

As Christians we need to follow and apply God's agenda. We rightly hate how homosexuality with its related deviancies and depravities is spreading and receiving increased general approval, and we rightly oppose the homosexual agenda. **But . . .** hating and opposing the homosexual *agenda* is one thing; how do we react to and come across to homosexual *people*?

That depends. For one thing, homosexuality is not just an issue with unbelievers and the loud, blatant, defiant perverters of God's truth, God's will. There are also many Christians who struggle with this sin silently. And that is a key word: *struggle*. They are aware of what God says on the subject, but they deal with a powerful inner force: sexual attraction to people of the same gender, an attraction that develops apart from their choice or desire. There is no settled science on just how or why this happens in some people; it is not from God, but it is in them. How do we deal with such people?

It is important that we start by acknowledging how *"sin so easily entangles"* each one of us also (Hebrews 12:1). We need to consider our own personal sinful weaknesses and inclinations: are we lazy, covetous and materialistic, envying, gossiping, lying, maliciously judging, lustful, indulging in heterosexual sins? Do we have "entangling" addictions in any such areas - not just drugs and alcohol? Then in that spiritual context of self-examination, confession and humility, *"let him who is without sin cast the first stone"* (John 8:7). Only in that framework are we qualified to approach the homosexual person whose sin we hate but whose soul we love.

Much has been well-written on the topic of this Christian approach to homosexuals. Since the concern at this point is simply to briefly consider this matter in the context of the hatred issues discussed here, see the list of selected resources at the close for further reading.

HATRED AND ISLAM

Another example: issues about Islam have become quite prominent in our time. (As with the term "homophobia", there is a corresponding term here: "Islamophobia"; the same misuse of the term and the same disclaimers apply here as there.) While on the one hand much of the American press, academia, and public opinion - and of course Islamic spokesmen - present Islam as a religion of peace, those who look behind this front find the actual facts to be a far different story.

So much about Islam properly arouses our righteous hatred: claims that Allah is but an alternate name for God; claims that the Koran's gross distortions of much of Biblical history, terminology, and theology somehow correct Christianity so that it can be absorbed into the lies of Islam; and of course true Islam's barbaric approach to life within its own culture, toward women especially, and toward what it calls "the Great Satan" outside of Islam. Islam's use of that term is so ironic, since it is hard to find a religion today that is more Satanic than Islam. A study of its Qu'ran and Haddith, plus a look at the revered (though grossly wicked and repugnant) life of Muhammad and the practices of Islam's most devoted followers easily justify that characterization.

But . . . here again, our initial approach to Muslim individuals, who also are blood-bought souls, cannot reflect our justified hatred of their religion. While Islam teaches its adherents to be duplicitous about their religion to non-Muslims, we can't let that fact obscure from us the fact that God's Word is more than capable of conquering their lies with His saving truth. While Islam teaches its people to hate, even kill Christians, we love Muslims and want to help them find life – now and forever. We know that our Lord loves these sinners also and wants us to at least attempt to not only tell Muslims about this Gospel love and salvation, but while doing so to model and reflect this love to them in person.

It is widely recognized that the percent of Muslims who adhere strictly to the Satanic teachings and prescribed practices of Islam and Muhammad may be "only" about 10 percent – which would still be around 150 million people world-wide. Thus there is the likelihood that individual Muslims we may encounter, especially here in America, may not be particularly duplicitous about their religion, may not actively hate Christians, may not be prone to violence, may not treat their women badly, and so on. Just as the majority of those in this world who identify as Christians have all too little knowledge and application of many of the teachings of Holy Scripture, so it is with Islam *in an opposite sense*. The majority of those who identify as Muslims, especially in Western countries, are reportedly at least somewhat unaware of the real teachings of their religion, or they disregard what they don't identify with, just as so many Christians disregard Scripture's teachings on matters such as creation, homosexuality, and the role of women in the church, because their world view doesn't match this "Word view". Many Muslims' Islamic identity is much more cultural, ethnic, traditional than it is theological, if we may use that term in this case.

This situation certainly works in our favor when relating to Muslims whom we may encounter. They may be more open to the Gospel than we expect. They may not have the family pressure and threats against conversion that is common in Islamic countries. And certainly the Gospel message itself can conquer, and has conquered, all of those negative factors even when they are present.

Here too, of course, a persistent, angry resistance to our witness, and possibly threats to our own selves, can justify our application of Jesus' words cited above, *"If anyone will not . . . listen to your words, shake the dust off your feet when you leave"* (Matthew 10:14). There are other blood-bought souls who will listen that the Lord will have no trouble leading in our direction.

The point here is that our justified hatred and proper criticism of the gross evils of Islam need not – and usually should not – color our approach to Muslim individuals. As with homosexuality, there is much well-written material about Islam and our interactions with Muslims, so please refer to the resources listed at the end here for further study.

HATRED AND EVOLUTION

One more example demonstrates another dimension of the point of this study. The Christian church has had to deal with the theory of evolution for over 150 years, so its dangers, its lies, can easily become so commonplace that we virtually ignore it. But a major, often-repeated warning in Scripture is summed up by Jesus' telling us to *"watch out for false prophets, who come to you in sheep's clothing but inwardly are ferocious wolves."* (Matthew 7:15) Being thus warned, ignoring or minimizing this false teaching is not an option for soldiers of the cross. And this lie is not only spread by unbelieving scientists, educators and media but unfortunately has gathered many adherents within the Christian Church, where too many naïve, deceived, or uninvolved sheep have fallen victim to these false prophets, to these wolves, for a long time.

The theory of evolution attacks not only the general truth of God's revelation in Holy Scripture, but it turns the foundational opening chapters of Scripture, in the book of Genesis, into mere man-made myths and legends, and claims that human science is more knowledgeable and truthful than the Word of God. Thus it undercuts the entire Christian faith. Because if God is not the Creator, not the One who made us and put us here, then are we really responsible to Him? If the fall into sin in the Garden of Eden is mere legend, then who really needs a real Savior from this mere mythical malady? And then also, of course, if this portion of God's Word would be mere human legend from ancient days of unscientific ignorance, how could we know that the remainder of the Bible does not also fit into that same category? We couldn't.

Does this not arouse our righteous hatred of this Satanic evil, this outrageous blasphemy? How dare anyone contradict almighty God! The hateful character of this denial of God's revealed truth is clearly a serious matter.

One reason that so many in the Christian church have fallen into this dangerous, entrapping error of evolution and its naturally consequent devastation of Christian doctrine is because of the too-common absence of a sense of seriousness, even urgency;

the absence of Godly hatred for this monstrous lie of Satan that insults our Lord and seriously attacks the faith of His people! Too many Christians just don't want to be bothered with "messy" doctrinal issues in general. And they pay little if any attention to what God tells us about hatred, as shown earlier, and how it is so important for us as we fight the good fight of the faith, certainly including this creation-evolution battle which we dare not ignore.

In this ongoing battle, we can thank God that He has blessed His people with many highly intelligent, very well-educated Christian scholars who are every bit as expert – sometimes more so – in the various branches of science as those who propagandize the Godless theory of evolution. These valuable servants have very well exposed the far-fetched speculation, the lies, the pseudo-science and the anti-Biblical bias of evolution, and they have clearly disarmed the arguments of evolutionists. These dedicated defenders of the faith have given us a treasure trove of most valuable resources to use as we expose the lies of Satan, as we struggle *"against the rulers, against the authorities, against the powers of this dark world and against the spiritual forces of evil in the heavenly realms."* (Ephesians 6:12) How well do we utilize these special gifts of God for ourselves, our loved ones, our friends and acquaintances, and thus ward off these attacks? See the references at the end of this study and equip yourself for this battle.

NO, IT'S NOT POLITICAL

When topics such as homosexuality, Islam, even evolution come up, it is not uncommon to hear Christians say, "Oh, I don't get involved in things like that; it's politics, and I try to avoid getting caught up in political debates." Or, "I like to keep church and state separate." While such intentions may be valid, the diagnosis is incorrect. These issues certainly have a political dimension, since they are frequent topics in the media and in political circles. But fundamentally they are spiritual, Biblical issues, as we've seen here. And if there is anyone who is most qualified to get involved in serious discussions of such matters, if there is anyone for whom they have the greatest impact, it is the Christian: the citizen who knows God's Word and who best appreciates the importance of these issues and the freedom – for himself or herself and for society in general - to live according to the will of our Lord.

The separation of church and state is a frequently misunderstood, often misapplied principle – though its detailed consideration is essentially beyond the scope of this discussion. But many issues in "politics" have a strong Scriptural dimension, certainly issues such as the three we have considered. So we need to be involved with them, giving our Christian witness, our faithful testimony. And when we're told that we are thus somehow mixing church and state, being "political", as it were, we can remind ourselves and others that we are simply being Biblical Christians, being salt and light. The political side of such issues is only incidental to us; the Scriptural side is fundamental.

Our collective voice as a congregation or church body faces legal restrictions on overt politically partisan words and actions; also, such words and actions can often be unwise, uncalled for and needlessly divisive, especially in mere civic, economic matters. But when political issues have a clear, unavoidable moral, Scriptural aspect, even our collective voice needs to be heard, avoiding legal violations when possible. And as individual Christian citizens we have more freedom to speak out than our church itself does, reflecting Scriptural principles in the public square. We know in advance that such testimony, such criticism, will be called "hate speech", but we love our Lord enough to speak up gladly in spite of that. Such speech needs to be careful, wise, sensitive – but not absent!

APPRECIATE THE CONTRAST

If we are in good health, live in a nice home in a good neighborhood, our family life is healthy and happy, and our finances and job are solid, it is easy for us to take this all for granted, to subconsciously assume that this is the general norm. But spend a day counseling deeply depressed or confused persons; spend a few days in a hospital, as a patient or even as a visitor; have strife develop in the family; spend a week in a poverty-ridden, politically dysfunctional and despotic country; spend a month suddenly and unexpectedly unemployed; and Wow! Those positive life factors, those blessings we took for granted, take on their true value for us, and our level of appreciation for them increases dramatically.

The same is true with the issues under consideration here. We need to recognize the tragic, evil, fatal contrasts to the truth of the Christian faith. We dare not flee the battles instead of fighting them. We dare not avoid facing the issues of our day because they are so "negative" or because people say that they're political matters, or because we think that they somehow don't affect the Gospel. We dare not miss out on such wonderful opportunities to grow in our appreciation of the supreme, most blessed treasure that is ours in not only the Gospel truth itself, but in all the attendant truths of God's Word that accompany it and that equip us to fight the good fight of the faith.

In other words, if we don't learn to properly hate the evil, the lies of Satan, how will we learn, by contrast, to properly love and appreciate the good, the glorious truths of God? We lose our sense of value for God's truth if we lack a firsthand encounter with or casually minimize its opposite, its enemy, the dire and dangerous threats against it. It is a key blessing for us to have a holy hatred for the evils in our world that are alive and active against us, including the evils of false teachings within the Christian church. That's because this is so vital for developing in us that natural counterpart: a much deeper, committed, energized and active appreciation for and devotion to the good, the truth that we are so privileged still to have in these dark days.

MISPLACED COMPASSION

Is there room for compassion toward those whose values we hate? Of course there is. And not simply on an individual level but also toward such classes of people whose collective defiance of God's will we hate. ***But . . .*** this is where so often confusion displaces confession. When a situation arises in which we must testify to God's condemnation of issues such as homosexuality, Islam, and evolution, the world is quick to broadcast its wrathful attacks on our testimony as being grievous and supposedly "un-Christian" hate speech. The world commands loud condemnation for us and our supposedly horrible, unfair, hateful treatment of such people, but at the same time it calls for great compassion and abundant support for the poor victims of our purportedly hateful words and general approach, no matter how gentle we have been.

At such times, for Christians who may not have been paying close enough attention – to the incident or the issue or to God's Word on such matters – similar feelings of compassion arise. While compassion toward those who are mistreated is good and natural for us as Christians, yet what happens too often in such cases is that this considerate compassion addresses the outward appearances of this alleged discrimination without getting to – or even considering – the defiant sinfulness that caused it and justifies it in the first place. That serious omission, that silence where testimony is needed, often appears to sanction what we dare not sanction. It is thus misplaced compassion.

The world intimidates – sometimes psychologically, sometimes physically – any who dare to address the underlying Biblical reasons involved in such situations. So often Christians capitulate to this intimidation, from fear and/or ignorance. This is why we need to *"Be self-controlled and alert. Your enemy the devil prowls around like a roaring lion, looking for someone to devour. Resist him, standing firm in the faith."* (1 Peter 5:8,9) And then in that firm stand and resisting faith we can proceed to *"speak the truth in love"* (Ephesians 4:15).

THE THREATS AND OUR RESPONSE

Christians living in so-called "Western Civilization" have learned from Scripture and from history in other places, at other times, of direct, physical persecution of Christians: how in the early years of the church they were thrown to the lions in Roman arenas, and how Christians have been imprisoned, beaten, tortured, beheaded and otherwise killed at other times and places. Read Hebrews 11:35-38, for example. But most of us in our own personal lives have not experienced this. And we thank God for that marvelous mercy.

This does not mean that such persecution cannot or will not return. From God's perspective, we know from history how His church, His people, have sometimes been at the strongest in their faith and their testimony during times of such direct persecution. From our contemporary earthly perspective, we can see how this persecution has again raised its ugly head so vigorously in recent times, especially under Islamic rule. It has been pointed out that there have been more executions of Christians in recent years than in all the previous history of the Christian church. Is this coming back for us, in our immediate future?

Only our Lord knows, of course. And there is no intent here to make any predictions along these lines. But if there is any area where we as Christians would appear to be most vulnerable to direct persecution in our day, it is in the area under discussion here: being charged with "hate speech", "hate crimes", being cited as a "hate group", and so on. Even when we simply give faithful, fair, loving testimony to Scripture's indictment of sinful attitudes and actions, the anti-Christian forces in our world react by equating this with the Godless words of sinful hatred and deeds of terrorism that spew forth from the ungodly. And they may soon charge us – in court, not just in the media – with hate crimes for such words; there are increasing signs of unsettling trends in this direction. In the short term, penalties for this can range from a revocation of tax-exempt status – a major financial impact on our ministries – to actual prison sentences, both of which are occurring today in Western societies. In the longer term, while only God knows when this more direct and dire persecution may actively re-surface in our midst, the lessons of history are not soothing. So now what? How will we act and react in such circumstances?

Our Lord nowhere commands us to *seek out* persecution. But He does tell us that persecution *will come*, in one way or another, at one time or another, if we live as His faithful witnesses, if we function as His salt and light: *"You will be handed over to be persecuted and put to death, and you will be hated by all nations because of Me."* (Matthew 24:9) So our role is to strike the proper balance here too. On the one hand, not needlessly soliciting persecution by going out of our way to invite confrontations when they may not be called for and could do unnecessary harm to our witness. But also not fearfully and faithlessly keeping quiet when our Lord wants us to speak up, testify to His will, even though our speech will be called "hate speech" for which there is a stiff penalty.

Already we've seen recent and growing evidence of such penalties, even in America. On the one hand, there are cases of what could be called "incidental persecution" from individual Islamists, or cases like the shooter in 2015 at a college in Oregon where those who professed Christ were killed on the spot. But then also there are incidents of more organized, sanctioned, legalized persecution: bakers, florists, photographers who withheld their services from events that celebrated homosexuality; a county clerk who refused to sign a homosexual "marriage" license; and others who lost their businesses, incurred massive fines, or were even imprisoned.

How will we respond when our testimony becomes suddenly very risky, in ways we have neither experienced nor expected? Will we be caught off guard and compromise under pressure? Will we let ourselves be bullied into silence? Or will we be ready and willing to continue a faithful testimony to God's truth even when such "hate speech" becomes quite costly? Clearly that second response depends on how firmly we are attached to our loving Lord, who alone is our *"refuge and strength, our ever-present help in trouble."* (Psalm 46:1)

WHAT ARE WE KNOWN FOR?

When dealing with matters that call for our internal hatred and external criticism, as we have examined here, the caution is often raised that it is important for us to be known for what we're *for*, not for what we're *against*. Good point. After all, do we as Christians, individually or collectively, want to be known as those who hate homosexuals, who hate Muslims, who hate evolutionists? Not only is that not true – we don't hate such *people* - but any righteous hatred we properly have about such *issues* is still not the whole focus of our faith, certainly not the foundation of the Gospel, and thus not what we want to be known for. ***But . . .*** that doesn't mean that we can just ignore or wrongly minimize these issues. Surely our Lord wants more than just a sad but silent *tsk, tsk* from us.

It is certainly possible to share, teach, preach the Gospel *as well as* to testify to the will of God in societal and personal issues. In fact, opening up discussion on these matters can provide a wonderful segue to the Gospel. For example, if people blame us for accusing or criticizing them, for hating them, we can not only humbly assure them that we also are sinners and that we do *not* hate them, but we can also counter their charges of hatred with the Gospel truth of God's love for them and for us all in spite of our sins, assuring them that Jesus' redemption covers all of their sins as well as all of ours. Thus the door is open for their repentance and faith, and the gate is open for them to Jesus' pastures.

As stated earlier, when particular evils arise in a prominent and dominant way in our world, our Christian voice – individually and collectively – dare not be silent, lest that silence be taken for tacit approval, consent. We heard God's question to us: *"Who will take a stand for Me against evildoers?"* (Psalm 94:16) St. Paul shows us how to answer: *"Put on the full armor of God so that when the day of evil comes you may be able to stand your ground. Stand firm, then, with the belt of truth, . . . the breastplate of righteousness, . . . the shield of faith, . . . the helmet of salvation, . . . and the sword of the Spirit, which is the Word of God."* (Ephesians 6:13-17)

SUMMARY

Yard signs have appeared that say - in English and five other languages - "Hatred has no home here". In many ways we as Christians can, should and do endorse that statement; but the point of this study has been to help us also know when we cannot, should not, and do not endorse it.

Do Christians hate? By God's grace and according to God's will, we most certainly do. Not in a sinful way but in a holy way. Not against God's will but according to God's will. We express our hatred of evil as criticism, yet we do not criticize in a destructive way but in a constructive, instructive, supportive and yes, loving way. After all, since Jesus died for us *"while we were still sinners"*, what can we do as His children but show our love for those whose sins we hate as He does, but whose souls we love as He also does?

St. Paul summarizes our Gospel motivation by saying, *"Christ's love compels us"* (2 Corinthians 5:14). In a somewhat ironic twist, we can also say, "Our hatred compels us." Certainly not a sinful, personal hatred; certainly not as a substitute for the ultimate compelling force of Christ's love for us sinners; but as a correlating compulsion. As we've seen, our hatred for what obstructs, contradicts, ignores, denies, defies God is not only a natural companion to our love for Him and our thankfulness for the precious blessings of His goodness and truth that we still possess, but it also thus *"compels us"*: it adds another important dimension to our Gospel motivation, to our determination to fight the evil and preserve the good at any cost. It instills in us the vital sense of *urgency* that these considerations call for. Our righteous hatred compels us to try to rescue those caught up in Satan's hateful lies because we love these people and thus attempt to lead them to God who *"**is** love"*, to their Savior who *"**is** the way, **the truth,** and the life"* (John 14:6), and who extends to them His hand of saving love. Thus our Godly hatred is a key partner with our Christ-centered love.

+   +   +

Jonathan Rupprecht is a graduate of Wisconsin Lutheran Seminary near Milwaukee, and served as a pastor for 23 years. He welcomes any comments, questions and discussion at jhr12447@aol.com .

+ + +

SELECTED FURTHER RESOURCES

General Apologetics:

Confronting Without Offending Deborah Smith Pegues
  Harvest House; Eugene, Oregon 2009 175 pages

The Defense Never Rests Craig A. Parton
Concordia Publishing House, St. Louis 2015 179 pages

I Don't Have Enough Faith to Be an Atheist
Norman L. Geisler and Frank Turek
Crossway Books; Wheaton, Illinois 2004 448 pages

A New Kind of Apologist Sean McDowell
Harvest House; Eugene, Oregon 2016 296 pages

Prepared to Answer Mark A. Paustian
Northwestern Publishing House, Milwaukee 2004 211 pages

More Prepared to Answer Mark A. Paustian
Northwestern Publishing House, Milwaukee 2004 242 pages

The Reason I Believe – The Basics of Christian Apologetics
Allen Quist
Concordia Publishing House, St. Louis 2017 194 pages

Your Questions, Scripture's Answers John F. Brug
Northwestern Publishing House, Milwaukee 2013 373 pages

Homosexuality:

Forgive Us Our Sins   Scott I. Barefoot and Richard D. Starr
Northwestern Publishing House, Milwaukee   2013   91 pages

Gay and God   Mike Novotny
Time of Grace Ministry, Milwaukee   2016   64 pages

Rainbow Savior   William A. Monday
WestBow Press; Bloomington, Indiana   2014   190 pages

Sexual Morality in a Christless Age   Matthew Rueger
Concordia Publishing House, St. Louis   2016   178 pages

Islam:

www.thestraightway.org   The web site of Usama Dakdok, a Christian Islamic expert who grew up in Egypt, albeit in a Christian home, but experienced and learned all the ins and outs of this religion. His site offers videos and books, including *"The Generous Quran"*, a more accurate translation than most, including helpful explanations and footnotes. He also travels around the US to give presentations. Usama exemplifies the love/hate dichotomy discussed here with the urgency that is clearly evident in his presentations.

Cross and Crescent – A Christian Introduction to Islam
Roland Cap Ehlke   Ehlke Works,   2016   59 pages

A God Who Hates   Wafa Sultan
St. Martin's Press, New York   2009   244 pages

Muslims – How to Respond   Ernest Hahn
Concordia Publishing House, St. Louis   2010   78 pages

Speaking the Truth in Love to Muslims   Roland Cap Ehlke
Northwestern Publishing House, Milwaukee   2004   219 pages

Evolution:

www.answersingenesis.org   A rich source of creation apologetics and related materials, from books to DVD's, presentations and visits to its Creation Museum and Ark Encounter near Cincinnati. Ken Ham is AiG's founder and president.

The Created Cosmos   Danny R. Faulkner
Master Books, 2016   352 pages

Evolution Impossible   John E. Ashton
Master Books   2012   196 pages

Faith and Science in a Skeptical Age   Jesse Yow, editor
Concordia Publishing House, St. Louis   2014   288 pages

www.ingramcontent.com/pod-product-compliance
Lightning Source LLC
Chambersburg PA
CBHW050609300426
44112CB00013B/2138